LIVE LIFE
SUNNY SIDE UP

JEREMYVILLE COMMUNITY SERVICE ANNOUNCEMENTS

Andrews McMeel
Publishing®

Kansas City · Sydney · London

INTRODUCTION

Thank you for picking up this book. In your palms you hold a cluster of tiny fragments and thoughts that I've collected along my winding path through this life.

I call them Community Service Announcements because I always imagined them as large street posters from a community initiative sanctioned by a fictitious, altruistic mayor of an imaginary town called Jeremyville. I see them as public messages for anyone who visits this town, walks past, and hopefully connects with these thoughts in some way. A message to change your day, even for just one quiet moment.

But this was never a planned project. It was only ever meant to be one single message.

It began one night around mid-2010, when I was chatting with a good friend who kept texting other people during our conversation. Disturbed by this very modern problem of being constantly hooked into electronics at the expense of real world relationships, that night I created a drawing to help me cope with how this made me feel. The drawing was titled "STOP TEXTING AND START CONNECTING," and it showed some friends sitting on a couch, disconnected from each other but engrossed in their smart phones. I added a small line beneath it: "This Has Been A Jeremyville Community Service Announcement."

I posted it to my social media that night and thought nothing else of it. I awoke to a flurry of Facebook likes and comments. This then encouraged me to create other messages in the hope of dealing with other concerns I was facing in life. There was an ongoing resonance within my social media network. The project snowballed from there, and if it were not for the constant connection with my supporters online, the project would have begun and ended with that one drawing long ago.

With my team of Megan and Neil from Studio Jeremyville, we now bring the CSA messages to cities around the world, from 300 paste-ups in the medieval Castle Estense in Ferrara, Italy, to CSA workshops in Oslo, Buenos Aires, Berlin, and São Paulo. We also have a New York City street newspaper, called *Jeremyville RAW*, which shares the CSA messages, and our Instagram account @Jeremyville—the best way to see firsthand a new CSA arriving into the world.

I have drawn about 800 messages so far, and create more in my sketchbook daily at my local cafe. This first compilation contains around 100 of my all-time favorites. I try to keep the messages as simple and sparse as possible, like a slightly opened door to welcome you inside. Please come in and feel at home, share some of your own history and experiences with the messages, and let them become a part of you. That is the ultimate aim for me—for the feelings to connect with you in a real, genuine, and very personal way.

We all need ways to reflect, contemplate, and enter into our own thoughts, like reading poetry, writing in a diary, or listening to an acoustic guitar played by a campfire. Here for you are some moments of introspection and quietness during the noise of your busy day.

With love,

Jeremyville
New York City

BE A
RANDOM ACT
OF KINDNESS.

TUNE IN TO
TODAY.

BE THE WIND
IN YOUR OWN SAIL.

MORE CUDDLES LESS TROUBLES.

STUFF
HAPPENS.

DON'T LET
LIFE
CUT YOU DOWN.

STAY TOGETHER.
WHATEVER.

BE YOURSELF
& NOBODY ELSE.

FILL YOUR LIFE
WITH MAGIC.

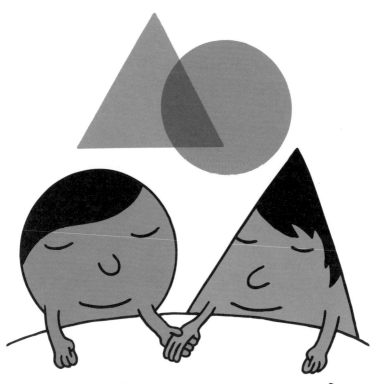

LET'S DREAM
OF EACH OTHER.

SPREAD HUGZ.

LIVE A BRIGHTER DAY.

FIND TRUE LOVE
WITH YOUR
EYES CLOSED.

DON'T LET ELECTRONICS COME BETWEEN US.

TAKE YOUR THOUGHTS FOR A WALK.

HOLD IT
TOGETHER.

DON'T TALK ABOUT IT. DO IT.

IT'S ALL A BEAUTIFUL JOURNEY.

LET YOUR HEART SHOW THE WAY.

ASK WHO OR WHAT
IS HOLDING YOU
BACK.

BE PATIENT.

BEST FRIENDS
FOREVER.

DON'T LET THE HATERS IN.

LET'S MEET ON
THE CORNER OF
TOMORROW &
FOREVER.

WALK ON THE
SUNNY SIDE OF LIFE.

TO END
IS TO BEGIN.

LET'S LEARN
TO SWITCH OFF.

FIX ME
DON'T DISCARD ME.

DON'T LET LIFE'S CHANCES SLIP AWAY.

FIND YOUR CLEARING
IN THE FOREST.

BECOME A CHAMPION OF YOUR OWN GAME.

DON'T LET
CONFORMITY
WEIGH YOU DOWN.

IMAGINE A DIFFERENT TOMORROW.

CALL HOME.

FEEL THE
LIGHTNESS
INSIDE YOU.

WHEN THIS WORLD
GETS YOU DOWN
FIND YOUR OUTSIDER TOWN.

DANCE FOREVER.

SAVE THE
SUNSHINE MOMENTS
FOR ANY
DARK DAYS AHEAD.

LET'S TWEET
THE OLD-FASHIONED WAY.

FIND YOUR PATH
TO THE SKY.

KEEP YOUR MIND OPEN
TO LIFE'S RANDOM SEEDS.

OWN YOUR STRANGENESS.

SPREAD LOVE.

TOMORROW
WILL BRING US
TOGETHER FOREVER.

IF LIFE GETS
SCRAMBLED,
TALK TO A FRIEND.

TRUST IN YOUR IDEAS AND JUMP.

CREATE MAGIK.

LIVE YOUR
DAYDREAM.

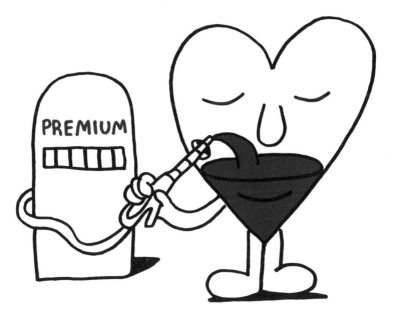

FILL UP
ON LOVE.

IMAGINE ETERNITY.

CREATE BY
MOONLIGHT.

DON'T FEAR
THE UNKNOWN.

LET'S SHARE
LIFE'S WAVE.

BE YOUR OWN GURU.

CATCH UP
WITH
OLD FRIENDS.

LET'S SPOON.

SLEEP SOLVES EVERYTHING.

LET DIFFERING
OPINIONS COEXIST.

FORGIVE.

HAVE A
WRINKLE FREE
DAY.

EACH YEAR
LIFE GETS
BRIGHTER.

DON'T WASTE
TOO MUCH TIME
ONLINE.

EMBRACE YOUR CITY.

FAT CAT, HELP THE ALLEY CAT.

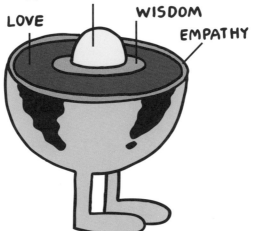

LOVE
ENLIGHTENMENT
WISDOM
EMPATHY

TRAVEL DEEPER INTO OURSELF.

GROUP HUG
YOURSELF.

CELEBRATE
ALL THE LAYERS
WITHIN YOU.

ESCAPE LIFE'S CUBICLE.

DRIFT AWAY
FROM THE EVERYDAY.

DON'T FOLLOW
THE TRENDS.

FIND YOUR
RAINBOW STAIRS.

LET'S SLIP
LIFE'S SKIN.

ENJOY THE SWEETNESS OF DOING NOTHING.

GET DOWN
STAY UP.

FORGET ABOUT
LIFE FOR A WHILE.

FROM TEARS,
CHANGES WILL GROW.

CREATE YOUR OWN TOMORROW.

DON'T GO
CHANGIN'.

LET'S GET CLOSER.

EAT MORE VEGETABLES.

HATERS
JUST NEED
A HUG.

BREAK DOWN
YOUR WALLS.

DON'T GET LOST ONLINE.

LET'S RADICALLY CHANGE OUR THINKING.

DO FEWER THINGS
AND DO THEM
BETTER.

DON'T LET LIFE GRIND YOU DOWN.

BUILD YOUR OASIS.

MARCH TO YOUR OWN TUNE.

STAY FREE
FOREVER.

LIVE IN THE LIGHT.

EVERYONE'S
IDEA OF FAMILY
IS DIFFERENT.

POLITENESS
IS LIKE
SUNSHINE.

WE ARE ALL ON
THIS ISLAND
TOGETHER.

YOU & ME
ON A JOURNEY
FOREVER.

IT'S OK TO BE
YOU
IT'S OK TO BE
ME.

WALK A MILE TO
FIND YOUR SMILE.

BUILD
YOUR OWN
RAINBOW.

FEEL THE ECSTASY
OF RAIN.

WITH YOU
I HAVE
EVERYTHING.

LIVE LIFE
SUNNY SIDE UP.

ACKNOWLEDGMENTS

I would like to especially thank these wonderful people: Jim Andrews, Patty Rice, Courtney Moilanen, and the team from Andrews McMeel Publishing, for being brave in publishing this first CSA book, and for having belief in the CSA message.

A giant bear hug also to uber talented author and longtime dear friend Bradley Trevor Greive, and to my dear literary agent Albert Zuckerman, founder of Writers House. These great people had a vision, joined the dots, and with their collective genius, made this all possible.

ABOUT THE AUTHOR

Jeremyville is a New York–based artist with an architecture degree from Sydney University. He shares his "Community Service Announcements" messages with the world, and on the streets of New York City, via his street newspaper *Jeremyville RAW*. His studio is based in a historic brownstone in Brooklyn, and he grew up by the ocean in Wonderland Avenue in Tamarama, a beachside suburb of Sydney, Australia.

Jeremyville has been exhibited at the Andy Warhol Museum in Pittsburgh, La Casa Encendida Museum in Madrid, the Madre Museum in Napoli, Colette in Paris, Cappellini in New York City, the 798 Arts District in Beijing, and is in many private collections around the world. Steven Heller, former art director at the *New York Times*, selected Jeremyville for his book *100 Illustrators*, published by Taschen.

Jeremyville is the co-founder of Studio Jeremyville, and has created projects for Converse, Swatch, Kiehl's, Uniqlo, Apple, Urban Outfitters, LeSportsac, Volkswagen, and Disney.

You can follow the Jeremyville Community Service Announcements on Instagram @Jeremyville and Facebook: www.facebook.com/ JeremyvilleDaily and at www.jeremyville.com.

This is his first compilation of the Community Service Announcements.

Andrews McMeel Publishing, LLC
an Andrews McMeel Universal company
1130 Walnut Street, Kansas City, Missouri 64106

www.andrewsmcmeel.com

15 16 17 18 19 TEN 10 9 8 7 6 5 4 3 2 1

ISBN: 978-1-4494-6685-5

Library of Congress Control Number: 2015930467